40 Inspirational Perspectives

of Reality

A Collection of Inspirational Messages to Help Individuals

Live Out Their Dreams

Roderick Hambrick

aka "The Acronymist"

40 Inspirational Perspectives of Reality:

A Collection of Inspirational Messages to Help Individuals Live Out Their Dreams

Copyright © 2022 by Roderick Hambrick

Printed in the United States of America.

Paperback ISBN: 979-8-9878738-1-6

Hardback ISBN: 979-8-9878738-2-3

eBook: 979-8-9878738-0-9

Acronymist Publishing

Terrell, Texas

Edited by: Naomi Books, LLC

I dedicate this book to my Lord and Savior, Jesus Christ,
who empowers me with the strength and courage
to step out of my comfort zone daily.

The Serenity Prayer

**God, grant me the serenity to accept
the things I cannot change,
the courage to change the things that I can,
and the wisdom to know the difference.
- Reinhold Niebuhr**

CONTENTS

ACKNOWLEDGMENTS

I am extremely grateful for all my family members who encouraged me while realizing the vision that was required to bring this book into existence. It all started as a hobby, but it was your love and support that made it reality. I started this process a couple of times in my life, but there was just something about this time that just… felt… right.

I thank my wife, Rusha, who understood the process of being inspired to write. Lord knows I would be up at the crack of dawn – all into the depths of night – constantly waking her up to give me feedback and watching her smile at me because of the questions I would ask.

Thanks to my brother, Ladarious, who gave praise to what he heard along the way as well as honest critiques to help mold the perfect message. I can see his face now, laughing, while stating that it could use a few curse words. He would listen to the words while at work and see its potential impact on every person.

They say that one can get into trouble for listing names, so I just want to send out big thanks to all individuals who have had a positive impact on my life – including the doubters.

40 INSPIRATIONAL PERSPECTIVES OF REALITY

This book was created as a means to decompress

40 years of knowledge coming hot off the press

How can something so basic achieve any kind of success

Just appealing to the masses who prefer 12 items or less

Who is this Acronymist person who nobody has ever heard?

It's a metaphorical person who redefines the power of words

Challenging everyone to reexamine their own perception

Asking you to come as you are... no need for any protection

Some of the things said in this book could offend you to the core

Bringing up topics that are taboo to discuss while leaving you wanting more

This is not me bragging or putting up some sort of hype

Reaching within myself to inspire the world about the realities of life

Some books are meant to be reread to find the hidden conclusion

Everyone will see something different, like an optical illusion

Before you turn to the next page and proceed to read

Don't forget to have an open mind to truly satisfy your curiosity

POINTS OF REFLECTION

I wanted to give the reader a canvass called, "Points of Reflection"

A place after each message where they can document introspections

It is said that change often comes after an uncomfortable resurrection

Waking up the mind, body, and spirit to conduct a necessary inspection

Cementing the foundation of change through thoughtful dissection

Helping the world become more aware of hateful infections

Letting them know we can always elect to make last-minute corrections

The secret glue has been within us all along, going by the name of "loving affection"

Most of us like to wait until things are just right with perfection

So, I am challenging all to meet me at the faith plus work intersection

Asking for an open mind and curiosity to overtake the concrete direction

I hope you take the time to enjoy a wonderful book and make all the abstract connections

EYES OF THE BEHOLDER

How we first met was just like fate

It was like The Man Above stretched out His arms saying, "checkmate."

Ever since that day you entered my life, people thought I was fake

Seems like others try to take you away by pointing out all my mistakes

Beauty's in the eyes of the beholder is the name of the game

Planting small seeds in life despite all the glory and fame

I won't stop grinding until the whole world knows

Even the eyes of the beholder change as success grows

Is this really a test... I guess

When much is given, comes much success

Am I really giving my best... Oh, yes

This must be my destiny... manifest

The fire within me will put others to rest, knowing I am blessed by the

best

I don't curse in my expressions, so I will say it real slow

Just like the movie, Last Dragon, took me a while to find the glow

I want to succeed so bad, just like it's my last breath

Leaving a legacy behind that supersedes my death

I know life is not all about pleasing man

Just a devoted father trying to show his children that they can

Hoping they gain the confidence to go after their dreams

Never forgetting where they come from amongst all the cheers and screams

For the eyes of the beholder never take a rest

It just merely passes on from one generation to the next

POINTS OF REFLECTION

1. Has anyone ever tried to minimize your worth by pointing out mistakes? Share.

2. Have you ever been tested to give an opportunity your best? Explain.

3. What is your motivation for success?

4. List three to five things you can do today to start shaping your journey.

ADDITIONAL THOUGHTS AND COMMENTS:

TRULY INSPIRED

Few ever thought I could become my best

Few ever thought I could pass their test

Protecting my dreams from negativity, so they won't become enmeshed

Empowering me with Your words of wisdom, so now I must confess

The roadblocks grew greater right before my very eyes

Just like the Garden of Eden, some were passion in disguise

But I knew I could count on You to give me the strength to rise

Using metaphorical expressions as dire lessons to bring society back to life

The most challenging turns ultimately evolve to self-doubt

But You and all Your glory did not count me out

The path least taken has stranded quite a few

Along this journey, I can hear a voice saying, "Son, it is bigger than you"

Inspiration is the motivation that drives the path

Staying steady on the road, despite the aftermath

Head up and chest out, saying, "thank you" to all my doubters

Because only what The Man Above says truly matters

POINTS OF REFLECTION

1. Who has previously told you (or who is currently telling you) that you can't succeed? What was your response?

2. What roadblocks stop you from realizing your true potential?

3. Have you ever doubted yourself? What got you through it?

ADDITIONAL THOUGHTS AND COMMENTS:

ENDANGERED SPECIES

"There are no good men out there," is the common phrase

But what we fail to realize is that one is literally born every day

How do I find them, or do they even exist

They are right in front of your eyes as soon as you abolish the list

Until we search deep within ourselves and fix our own insecurities

You will continue to battle the same foe until you realize the enemy is "me"

Instead of projecting them onto everyone else

Search for common unity by loving yourself

For the endangered species is merely a myth

It is just our own imperfections trying to find the perfect fit

Ladies, when you find the one

Never let them go

For the endangered species may come once a lifetime

Then you can let the whole world know

POINTS OF REFLECTION

1. Have you ever thought that a good partner did not exist?

2. Write out the real or imagined list you created for your potential mate.

3. Compare yourself to those expectations and desires for your partner.

4. Often, we find it's our own insecurities trying to find the perfect fit. What are some of your insecurities?

5. Identify three to five things you can do to address your personal insecurities.

ADDITIONAL THOUGHTS AND COMMENTS:

THROUGH THE DARKNESS

Through the darkness, I saw the light

Praying for a sign, but there was nothing in sight

The strength I had was there all along

Just waiting to be discovered and claim my throne

Faith is more than just a five-letter word

It was not until I decided to open my eyes to realize its true worth

Accepting the things that I cannot change

Lord, why must we endure all this agony and pain

Relax, this too shall pass, for it is only a test

Be patient and still because God knows best

Although this darkness can be an overwhelming sight

Remember, there is a darkening process before the fruit is ripe

"There's always light at the end of the tunnel," is a common cliché

For there is wisdom in darkness if we just stay the course

The answer is to have faith and pray each day

Because life is too short for remorse

POINTS OF REFLECTION

1. What has been one of the darkest moments for you?

2. How did you remain strong to make it to the light at the other end of the tunnel?

3. Think of three to five activities you can do to appreciate life's hidden treasures without feelings of guilt or remorse.

ADDITIONAL THOUGHTS AND COMMENTS:

PLAGUES OF INSECURITY

What is this feeling that makes me question myself

It's like winning a championship without the belt

In my eyes, I can do no wrong

Until the feeling makes me wonder if I even belong

Insecurity is the emotion that causes distress

It is the underlying belief that I can't measure up to the rest

I know everyone is different in their own special way

The thought, "I should be better" plagues many every day

For this emotion can cause a lifetime of blame

If we look deep into our past, we can find the origin from which it came

Let's not project this blame onto our loved ones

Because they are the key to help us overcome

The answer is understanding that we all have flaws

Nobody is perfect or must abide by unwritten laws

Just trust in the process of loving yourself

Sound body and mind are essential to our health

The opposite is feeling secure

There are no uncertainties just being assured

I know this sounds like a fairy tale to most

Becoming the best you does not require one to brag and boast

It is merely living your life truly inspired

While eliminating distractions that block your fire

For it can be challenging to withstand the tests of time

Our true potential is revealed when thoughts, emotions, and attitudes align

POINTS OF REFLECTION

1. Have you ever felt insecure about your purpose in life? Explain.

2. What were some thoughts that have plagued your mind?

3. How did these thoughts impact relationships with family and friends?

4. Write out three to five positive affirmations that can counter future thoughts of insecurity.

ADDITIONAL THOUGHTS AND COMMENTS:

COLD SHOULDER

In the inception, there was just one
Who believed in something so great
When I was starving to achieve
You were there to keep me straight

Sounds like a great idea
Everyone would say
Until the day of the cold shoulder
I learned I had to do it my way

So, I focused on my journey
Dotting my i's and crossing my t's
Little did I know that the cold shoulder
Would find a problem with me

What is a cold shoulder

It is a young mind that refuses to get older

There is a lack of understanding on the rationale for such tasks

For my plan was built by the Highest to stand strong around all the
masks

Not if, but when, you experience the cold shoulder

Just remember overcoming obstacles is what makes us bolder

Higher plans are not meant to be understood

Behind every cold shoulder is someone who wishes they could

POINTS OF REFLECTION

1. Tell me about a time when you got excited about an opportunity, but received the cold shoulder.

2. What did you learn about yourself during this experience?

3. Share two or three ways you would handle a cold shoulder today.

ADDITIONAL THOUGHTS AND COMMENTS:

WISHFUL THINKING

They say a dream is merely a plan with no action

A wish is simply direction with no traction

How is it that we wish for things we never had

With hard work and persistence, anyone can grab the bag

For it is easier to wish than to put in hard work

Truth is... entitlement makes us feel like we deserve

When much is given, much is required

Most of us are so ready to give up and retire

Therefore, we give up and come up with different mottos

We invest less in ourselves, but more into the lotto

Reality is that we believe we can't

We disregard our talents while focusing on ain'ts

Continue to wish upon a falling star

The star is falling for a reason because we are not being true to who we

are

POINTS OF REFLECTION

1. What is something you always wished for?

2. What were some mottos or rationalizations you came up with to excuse your lack of action?

3. Name three to five new mottos that can keep you action-oriented toward your dreams and aspirations.

ADDITIONAL THOUGHTS AND COMMENTS:

UNEXPLAINABLE GIFT

Rise up, rise up. Oh, what a day

I see a gift with my name on it in a special way

What is it in this small box

Oh, my dear. I hope it is not socks

So, I pick up the gift but there was no sender

Was it for my birthday or a special occasion? I don't remember

I grab it, shake it, and move it all about

Just like the Hokey Pokey and turn myself around

It was time to open it or maybe take a peek

Who would send an unexplainable gift with so much mystery

The ecstatic look upon my face was such a sight to see

It was absolutely wrapped perfectly, just like it was meant for me

Searching for our gift is a discovery that can be lifelong

If we look closely in the box, it has been with us all along

POINTS OF REFLECTION

1. Write about a moment when you were searching for a gift that was within you all along.

ADDITIONAL THOUGHTS AND COMMENTS:

BECOMING A LEGEND

Letting everyone know my every move

Pure anger toward themselves because there is nothing they can do

Wishing that I fail, give up, or hang 'em up on the shelf

But why quit now when there is so much left

The legacy I am leaving is bigger than me or you

Before passing judgment, just take a moment to walk in my shoes

Don't take it personally when a legend says how they feel

Reinventing yourself does not involve changing the wheel

Most legends don't speak much unless it is facts

If you want to become a legend, just follow the act

For it is one's duty to keep it real no matter how hard it gets

Daring anyone to stop me from achieving my success

Legendary status is not self-proclaimed but recognized by others

Everyone acknowledges your work from children to mothers

Let's not get lost in the people calling your name

For true glory comes when we give credit to the process and evolve, never

being the same

POINTS OF REFLECTION

1. Have you ever had the desire to become the best at what you do? What was it?

2. Who were some of your biggest critics?

3. How did you evolve your mindset to make room for the abundance of success?

4. What struggles did you have in the maintenance stage of success?

5. Write a brief letter to all the haters, doubters, and future dream pursuers.

ADDITIONAL THOUGHTS AND COMMENTS:

IT'S MY TIME

Have you ever felt like you were meant to do much more

Then the next day awake wondering if life is worth fighting for

The battle of ambivalence can be one big test

Answer is surrendering to your destiny to become your best

Ever seem like there are no right tasks for you

Maybe we are trying to be too cute by putting on small shoes

For your destiny awaits when you take the first step

Stating that it's my time while following the Word... nothing else

Maybe I'll wait till I get my life just right

Give me one more day and another night

Before we know it, so much time passes by

We lose our fight and our will to try

Take action while trusting in yourself

For you will be taken to higher heights with every breath

Be aware of the blockers that get in your way

It is just someone who has put off their time and wished for better days

POINTS OF REFLECTION

1.   Tell me about that special moment when you realized you were meant to do much more.

2.   How did you deal with ambivalence or indecisiveness?

3.   What made you ultimately decide to push fear aside?

4.   Give three to five lines of encouragement to others who may be "stuck" on their journey.

ADDITIONAL THOUGHTS AND COMMENTS:

ANXIETY

What is this feeling that makes me feel such a mess

It is like my mind and body are in a race to see who's best

Constant worries about things beyond my control

Could someone please slow it down or just pay the toll

My emotions are all over the place, which is so hard to explain

Just like a child in the elevator pushing buttons on my brain

Life gets so out of control making it hard to prioritize

Overwhelmed with exhaustion, so I just cover my very eyes

Don't let me get started with a little irritation in the mix

I will go off the handle like a crossover, game point... who's next

So, if you ever wonder why I am not acting like me

I would like to introduce you to my nemesis, named anxiety

POINTS OF REFLECTION

1. How has anxiety played a role in keeping you from reaching life's goals and milestones?

2. Describe some of the symptoms you either personally experienced or witnessed with someone else.

3. Name three creative ways you learned how to cope with these symptoms.

ADDITIONAL THOUGHTS AND COMMENTS:

MESSENGER

How is it that I can say the same thing they just said

Because of my stature around the people, my knowledge gets left on red

Is it the delay of my success

Sometimes the best words of wisdom come from those who have less

Charge it to their heads and not the heart

I knew the Lord was using me from the very start

The messenger can come when we least expect

Be ready for your message without disrespect

We get so busy blocking the message by worrying about our attire

For the messenger is sent from a higher place to help you regain your fire

Please look high and low for messages around you every day

The one who you overlook may be the one who paves your way

POINTS OF REFLECTION

1. Has anyone ever disregarded your words because of success's delay? Explain.

2. Describe a time when you received a life-changing message from someone who had less.

3. What message do you feel you must share with the world?

4. Identify three ways you can start becoming more intentional with your message today.

ADDITIONAL THOUGHTS AND COMMENTS:

PERFECTLY IMPERFECT

No matter how hard we try to please, we will keep falling short

Most of them pointing out my flaws just like it was a sport

Looking for ways to be entertained

Attacking my character for personal gain

Being perfect is an insurmountable task

Walking around everybody wondering... which mask

Why do we put so much energy into pleasing others

These are the same ones who take pleasure in watching us smother

Perfectly imperfect means loving every part of you

From the top of your head to the soles of your shoes

True beauty is said to come from within

Our negative thoughts about ourselves stick out like a pimple just
breaking skin

So, loving yourself is what creates the rep

We teach others how to treat us... nobody else

Become the true teacher of Y-O-U

Because nobody loves me like I do

POINTS OF REFLECTION

1. Share a moment when you felt like you had to be perfect for others

    to notice you.

2. What different masks have you worn to please others?

3. How did it feel when the same efforts were not given back to you?

4. List three to five ways to find peace in being perfectly imperfect.

ADDITIONAL THOUGHTS AND COMMENTS:

W - L

Is there really such a thing as a win and a loss

Some strongly believe in winning at any cost

Winning is good on many occasions

It does not matter if you are Black, White, Hispanic, or Asian

How can one go through life without ever experiencing a loss

It is the mighty power of perception... who is the boss

Perception is being aware of different interpretations

Which starts by opening your mind to new information

Instead, let's turn the L's to lessons

Please believe that this is not a confession

Because one does not truly lose unless they forgo the learning process

History has proven that L's are steps along the road to success

So, pick your head up and push through these learning experiences

Steady lessons are the true key to developing a champion spirit

POINTS OF REFLECTION

1. Do you think someone can go through life without experiencing a loss? Why or why not?

2. What makes it difficult or easy for you to see losses as lessons?

3. Tell me about a time when you learned more from a lesson than a win.

ADDITIONAL THOUGHTS AND COMMENTS:

IMPULSES

Jumping, clamoring, and acting without a thought

I love this feeling because I won't get caught

Constantly sabotaging my own success

I did not get it this time; there will always be the next

Maybe they won't see or have the time

How can I be guilty of a victimless crime

The only one affected is just myself

I have been this way all along without any help

I don't see any problem with me doing me

The absence of thought in our actions is called, "impulsivity"

Feelings override your every move

Truth is... you have lost touch with the real you

Continuing your ways will bring a world of pain

All the lying, shouting, crying, has only one to blame

Don't feel sorry when others treat you black and blue

Until you break the cycle, trouble will always stick like glue

POINTS OF REFLECTION

1. Have you ever been stuck in an impulsive cycle? Share.

2. What were some of your daily struggles that kept you in the cycle?

3. List some ways you were able to break the cycle.

4. Identify three to five things you can do to keep the cycle from repeating itself in future generations.

ADDITIONAL THOUGHTS AND COMMENTS:

INFLUENCES

Trying to find my identity in this world we live in today

Seems like negativity is constantly around us, claiming it's the way

Seeing individuals laugh at other people's pain

It's like positivity is now considered Plain Jane

The success of social media has provided little to no hope

Negativity spreading like wildfire with few ways to cope

Everyone's an advice giver to make it through the struggle

But the real power comes when we love one another

Not all influences are designed to bring so much shame

Seek out positive influences and change the game

For it is long overdue for positive individuals to stand up

Don't wait for issues to hit your doorstep, then try to erupt

They say only love can conquer hate

So, let's not sit still on the sidelines saying, "I'm straight"

Invest in the youth to fix society like a suture

The product will be a brighter future

POINTS OF REFLECTION

1. How has negativity impacted your ability to discover your identity?

2. Identify three to five positive influences in your life.

ADDITIONAL THOUGHTS AND COMMENTS:

PRIDE

Too much, too little, got to find that equilibrium

It's like getting taken out of the game too early... hard to find a rhythm

What is this thing that gets me stalemated in all my thoughts

So hard to put my finger on it, but I will not give in at any cost

The word is pride that makes me hide all my hopes and dreams

For if the idea was born from someone else, I can't internalize it and still be me

Truth is... few have come up with original ideas by themselves

If you look deep into the context, you will find the remnants of someone else

This is not a testament to live a life without pride

Just keep it in check to reach your potential and truly rise

Pride in moderation is always best

Implement this philosophy to maximize your success

POINTS OF REFLECTION

1. How has too much or too little pride prevented you from reaching
    your potential?

2. Share three ways you can keep your pride in check today.

ADDITIONAL THOUGHTS AND COMMENTS:

CREATIVE

Being creative is a wonderful choice

Just like a singer discovering their voice

It is so easy to leave everything plain

The more creative one gets, comes more complaints

People will try to knock you out the sky

Which makes it so important to develop a strong why

The next step is to educate yourself

Then start to take action like there is nothing left

They say when one gains knowledge, with it comes power

The lack of application makes room for the devour

So don't lose that vision, keep it the main feature

Keep evaluating the process because one day the student becomes the

teacher

POINTS OF REFLECTION

1.   What complaints have you heard when trying to get more creative?

2.   State three to five things you can do today to prepare youth to be suitable teachers.

ADDITIONAL THOUGHTS AND COMMENTS:

EARLY RETIREMENT

I don't feel like I can remain in this place

It is like the weight of the world is taking over my mental space

Just looking around trying to find a connection

Seems like every day is another rejection

Can't feel anything, like my body is getting numb

Hoping finally that one day would come

It hurts me so badly to stay alive

Never thought the day would come that I contemplate suicide

Maybe someone else could end my reign

Kind of like the biblical tales of Able and Cain

Will I go to heaven or maybe straight to hell

Hell is probably better than this; only time will tell

Needing a way to escape all this pain

Retire my jersey before my prime and walk away from the game

Not being in control of my life is driving me insane

Maybe after this, someone will finally remember my name

Truth is... this will be a big loss down to its very word

The pain does not really escape; it is merely transferred

This world could be a very complicated place

Look for positive motivation to stay in the race

There will always be things in life that we don't understand

Control what we can control is the master plan

Just when we think that we have nothing else left

Find solace in a higher power and don't be afraid to ask for help

POINTS OF REFLECTION

1. Have you ever felt like the weight of the world takes over your mental space? Explain.

2. Has the thought of suicide crossed your mind?

3. If so, what led you to consider this permanent solution?

4. List three to five names and phone numbers of people you can contact to talk about your plan to remain safe.

(National Suicide Hotline 1-800-799-7233)

ADDITIONAL THOUGHTS AND COMMENTS:

DEAR FATHER

Father, I stretch my arms to thee

Not knowing that your face would not be the one I see

The world seems so bright, which makes my vision a total mess

Then I was placed in mother's arms, closing my eyes to rest

I thought I would see you the very next day

But all I see is mother sitting to pray

Wondering why you did not see my first step

Not realizing that mom was not the only one you left

So, I am now searching for someone that can be a father figure

Lost all trust in man... now my hands are on the trigger

Not thinking twice about life because it was not given to me

Don't care about myself or even humanity

Father, before you think about walking away

The love you give now prevents most monsters today

Let's stop letting mothers front the bill without help

The world would be a greater place if we give less priority to self.

POINTS OF REFLECTION

1. Who was the father figure in your life?

2. How did his presence or absence impact your life?

3. What are some things you would have liked to learn from him?

4. List some ways you can become a better father for your current or future children. Or share from your experience with your own father.

ADDITIONAL THOUGHTS AND COMMENTS:

EXCUSES

My ego is so fragile that it gives other people the blues

Instead of learning from my mistakes, I rather make an excuse

No matter which path I take... I can't stand to lose

The mere thought of someone defeating me... I down right refuse

It gets hard accepting responsibility for the things that I do

You are my best defense of keeping composure while staying cool

Issuing them all out like a stimulus check

Overdependent on the power while leaving my life a complete wreck

Take a close look at what you need to do

Accept the lessons as reminders to stay true

For making excuses will eventually catch up... only time will tell

The very person receiving the excuse will be needed for your bail

When we cry wolf for so long and finally get captured

There will be no mercy, like a sinner caught in the rapture

POINTS OF REFLECTION

1. Do you make excuses? Why?

2. How do you feel excuses impact society today?

3. Tell me about a time when you made an excuse.

4. Identify three to five positive statements that can counter excuse making.

ADDITIONAL THOUGHTS AND COMMENTS:

MIRROR

Staring at my reflection... what do I see

There is something wrong with my hair, skin, and teeth

I don't like what I see right before my very eyes

Somebody's playing with the mirror because this can't be right

Trying different looks, but nothing seems to match up

Even thought about considering some nip and tuck

If beauty really is skin deep,

Then maybe I can get past this first layer to find the real me

Truth is... the real mirror is society

Trying to define you and tell you what to be

The Creator made you different and very unique

Let's not change our image for the moment like X-Men's Mystique

Just smile at all your flaws and imperfections

Because our children will be our final reflection

POINTS OF REFLECTION

1. What do you see when looking at your reflection in the mirror?

2. Have you ever considered physically changing a part of yourself? If so, what?

3. What are some insecure thoughts you have about your natural self?

4. State three to five things about your physical appearance which you consider beautiful.

ADDITIONAL THOUGHTS AND COMMENTS:

THE ONE THAT GOT AWAY

Just like a bird in a cage unable to spread its wings

Taking for granted all the joy you bring

So afraid to let you fly out of my sight

Because deep down I was scared to soar to new heights

You would tell me all about your dreams

But I was more interested in keeping you on a string

I knew your cage would open one day

Begging and pleading but you would not stay

Now, I see the Master has bigger plans

You were meant to see the moon while I play in the sand

I guess there were some things that you made me see

Finally realizing that the caged bird is really me

POINTS OF REFLECTION

1. Has there ever been someone or something that got away? Explain.

2. What role did you play in its loss?

3. If you could go back in time, what would you have done differently?

4. Share three ways you can prevent history from repeating itself in the future.

ADDITIONAL THOUGHTS AND COMMENTS:

GATEKEEPER

He said, "I love you" on the very first date

Kind of like a scene in the movie, Can't Hardly Wait

For you are the gatekeeper for the fountain of unity

The key is a lifetime gift... not meant for promiscuity

Maybe he will find the key to another gate

Look deep within yourself, stating you are well worth the wait

They may try to sneak the key away by pulling the wool over your eyes

Trying to play on your emotions, so child, don't be surprised

Anything worth having is worth working for

Become the Neiman Marcus, not the convenient store

The standards you set will weed out all the pests

That prey on the weak who will settle for less

Your body is a temple to be truly adored

Command more from these bums because the power has always been yours

POINTS OF REFLECTION

1. What is the most powerful thing you possess?

2. Have you ever felt pressured to do something you did not want to do? Explain.

3. Identify three to five ways you can restore the power of self-love.

ADDITIONAL THOUGHTS AND COMMENTS:

DRAFT

The path to success is just like an NFL draft

Teams that underachieve get the biggest return... no cap

Follow the motto of "united we stand"

Just like Michael, become a superstar and break away from the band

Staying in a vicious cycle like a hamster in a wheel

Every year using opportunity funds just to pay bills

Got to keep it real is the only way I got to be

Lack of motivation and education equals poverty

They say insanity is doing the same thing over again expecting different
results

The refusal to elevate your mind is like having screws and no bolts

Taking government benefits over time, moving like a snail

Setting up traps like PPP loans, knowing you will grab it and fail

Take your power back People and get off the list

Championships are never won constantly getting the first pick

POINTS OF REFLECTION

1.   Does your life ever feel like a hamster wheel? Share.

2.   State three to five things you can do today to begin the process of breaking the cycle of poverty.

ADDITIONAL THOUGHTS AND COMMENTS:

COMFORT ZONE

I don't ever want to leave the confines of this place

Like an institutionalized prisoner catching another case

Living high on the hog... you know, stress free

While the underutilization of my talents diminishes... atrophy

This is all I know; it is what I call home

You can't make me evacuate this thing called, "the comfort zone"

Stay on the porch and don't ignore what we are trying to say

Nobody tells me what to do in my zone... Section 8

If you ever try to leave your zone

Find a good mentor that sets the tone

You will find that this world could be an awesome place

When you finally wake up and decide to turn the page

There are so many things that you can do

Never looking back now that we have a clue

Knowing that it can be scary but safe to roam

For I know I am covered to fully receive my throne

POINTS OF REFLECTION

1. Describe situations that make you feel comfortable.

2. How do you know when you are become too comfortable with something?

3. Discuss three to five ways you can challenge yourself to get out of life's many comfort zones.

ADDITIONAL THOUGHTS AND COMMENTS:

JUSTICE

So tired of losing, thinking one day I will win

Facing a juggernaut enemy... the color of my skin

I show them mercy and even grace

Instead of looking in my heart, they can't see past my face

They say the true color of justice is green

Calling me out my name, hoping that I cause a scene

Speaking out to say that we matter has grown quite grotesque

Not saying we are better, just asking not to get treated like we are less

Don't let the acts of a few ruin it for multiple generations

Are we really seeking change or just merely contemplation

Patting ourselves on the back while balancing checkbooks

Sacrificing the life of another like a game of chess and I am the rook

Stand up, my People; a change gon' come

For we must all finally answer for the wrong we have done

This too shall pass, so let's pray for the best

Our faith has always gotten us through... heads up, be blessed

POINTS OF REFLECTION

1. How do you deal with injustice today?

2. Do you ever feel as if you get blamed for another person's mistakes? Explain.

3. What do you think we can do to bring more equality to the justice system?

4. List three to five ways you can become a part of the change you want to see in the justice system.

ADDITIONAL THOUGHTS AND COMMENTS:

SUCCESS

I got that "S" on my chest, feeling like I am the man

Bittersweet depends on how you see it... cinnamon

So tired of walking through life with a lot of regrets

Hoping for the day I don't have to live check to check

Constantly feeling like I got something to prove

Took me a long time to get at this table, so I am going to enjoy my food

Some may think I was lucky or maybe just very smart

Success starts in the mind and eventually moves to the heart

Never settling for anything less than my best

Is the mindset that has no time for excuses or disrespects

Get to the point where you are serving plates to guests

For true success comes when doors get knocked down for the rest

POINTS OF REFLECTION

1.   What is your definition of success?

2.   What prevents you from becoming successful?

3.   Share three positive statements that can jumpstart your success.

ADDITIONAL THOUGHTS AND COMMENTS:

ROLE MODELS

They say that actions speak louder than words

I thought "words" was a noun and not a verb

So busy telling other people what to do

When we don't even walk a mile in our very own shoes

It's like we start to preach before we practice

Yeah, I heard of that profession before; I think it's called, "acting"

Eager to lead and expect others to follow

Choking on our own words while wanting everyone else to swallow

Ready to fight when someone questions your quest

Pointing all the attention away from you know who – guess

Some of you may be thinking I am spitting all kinds of hate

Just another guy blocking and throwing a lot of shade

Becoming a positive role model has no room for the fake

Conducting yourself like someone's always watching while owning up to

your mistakes

Teflon to criticism cause my walk is my confession

Of how a positive role model impacts the community – no question

POINTS OF REFLECTION

1. Who is your biggest role model?

2. What traits do you admire about this person?

3. What influences do they have on your life and your decision-making?

4. List some ways you can become a positive role model for the next generation.

ADDITIONAL THOUGHTS AND COMMENTS:

PRIVACY

You said you love me as we walked down the aisle

Smiling at you, thinking, I can't wait to bear your child

Telling everyone the night before... this will be the best day of my life

Little did I know – I would have to think twice

I made all the excuses for the ways you behaved

Not realizing that I was digging myself an early grave

You did it because you loved me, is what you said

Is love supposed to hurt or maybe I'm just sick in the head

Stuck around through all your mess

Even watched you plagiarize my own success

I have coached my friends through similar situations

But now it's happening to me, so I avoid conversation

Decided to speak out against this crime

Said I was not going back... again I lied

Now I fully understand how love is blind

Guilt trips, manipulation, and religious beliefs twist your mind

One day I was finally able to get away

Reinvented myself by discovering my talents, supports, and ability to pray

For all the individuals who suffer in silence

Surround yourself with support and give negativity the Heisman

The loss of a loved one by any means can be a horrible sight to see

Make sure you don't become a victim of the thing called privacy.

POINTS OF REFLECTION

1. Has privacy ever come back to haunt you? If so, how?

2. What were some childhood sayings you heard about privacy?

3. Have you ever lost someone due to privacy? Share.

4.   Name five warning signs that a friend or loved one tries to hide when dealing with privacy.

5.   Identify three to five ways you can stop privacy from claiming another victim.

(National Domestic Violence Hotline 1-800-799-7233)

ADDITIONAL THOUGHTS AND COMMENTS:

RESTORATION PROJECT

Some days I feel so good that I just want to shout

Then get inside my own head listening to all the clout

I have done this a thousand times, when it was only just me

Feel like I am in a pressure cooker with the contents on steam

This is the moment you have been waiting for – don't get lost in the crowd

Just like I knew it, was surrounded by doubt

Would they like what I have to say

A beacon of inspiration... nah, no way

What if they judge me by my surface

I don't know what's cool now... maybe down to earth is

People tell me I should just be myself

Just relax and play the game as if there were no refs

How can others believe if I don't believe in me

Success comes when preparation meets opportunity

Thank you, doubt, for prepping me to be my very best

For anyone who can't accept the real me, you can leave my set

POINTS OF REFLECTION

1. Tell me about a situation when you were surrounded by doubt?

2. What were the thoughts that caused those feelings?

3. State three to five ways you have overcome doubt in the past or how you are currently overcoming doubt.

ADDITIONAL THOUGHTS AND COMMENTS:

COVERT OPERATION

They say good things come to those who wait

How come every time I want something, You are always late

It may not come when you want it, but it is always on time

I will just weed out the middleman and get it done faster online

I have been so good and stayed the course

Even praised Your Name until my voice became hoarse

Feeling like I am throwing quarters into a wishing well

Waiting on that special call, but it turns out to be another sell

Wanting others to be patient with us, but give no time to others

Come up with all the excuses in the world, but they all just sound like
stutters

Being patient is the name of the process

Don't rush it unless you plan to overpay for less

Take the time and consider a better strategy

Like showing congruence, unconditional positive regard, and empathy

For we may not know what another person is going through

Give each other a break because the next person could be you

POINTS OF REFLECTION

1. Tell me about a time when you questioned why you had to wait for something.

2. Do you have a tendency to want others to be patient with you, but you are not patient with them? Share.

3. What has being impatient cost you in the long run?

4. Identify three to five ways you practice having patience today.

ADDITIONAL THOUGHTS AND COMMENTS:

TRANSITIONS

I want to change, but I don't think I can

Tried that commitment thing but just like a person with cold feet – I ran

I keep telling myself that I still got time

Even though I see people losing their lives daily to these foolish crimes

Momma always told me there would be days like this

Paying little attention to what she said until that day I got a kid

Still stubborn and staying out at all times of the night

Constantly denying I was addicted to my first child, the fast life

Pledged my life every day to these streets

Wait... commitment has always been there like a game of hide-n-seek

How do I change something that has such a big hold?

Admitting there is a problem while allowing your higher power to be the
mold

They say the first step is always the hardest to do

Overcoming this step will allow many individuals to see your testimony

as living proof

Just believe in your mind that change is possible

Have faith the size of a mustard seed and you will become unstoppable

There will be many distractions that come along your journey

The change you make today will impact you for an eternity

POINTS OF REFLECTION

1.   What was the turning point that allowed you to see a transition was needed?

2.   Name three to five excuses that kept you stuck in self-defeating behaviors.

3.   List three things you can do today that can allow you to overcome your prior history.

ADDITIONAL THOUGHTS AND COMMENTS:

ETERNALLY GRATEFUL

You believed in me all along when I did not even try

Maybe it's not my season or the well was dry

Stood there by my side chanting that I will make it

Pushing me beyond my limits, therefore your love will never be forsaken

Praise me for all my rights while calling out my wrongs

Even though I can't see you, your voice beckons in my head like an addictive song

During our last meeting, I knew you were not at your best

Putting on a smile for everyone still treating them like your guest

You were there with me through all my trials

All the challenging relationships – Girls Gone Wild

Teacher of many, the eliminator of stress

Nothing was ever too big to get off my chest

Wishing you were here to see this small seed grow into a tree

I can't talk to your face, so I contact you spiritually

Letting you know what a great job you have done

Preparing me for the greatest victories, but the real work has just begun

There are so many others that were not privileged to have someone like you

Praying for a savior that can show them all the right moves

Your life lives on through me to help light the way

Let's stop putting off tomorrow and focus on what we can do today

POINTS OF REFLECTION

1. Who is the person for whom you are eternally grateful (living or deceased)?

2. How did this person impact your life?

3. If this person were in front of you now, what would you say - in three sentences?

4. List three to five ways you can keep this person's memory alive and with you today.

ADDITIONAL THOUGHTS AND COMMENTS:

UNTOLD STORY

It started out being so much fun, a beautiful sight to see

I saw the love in your eyes, so I knew I had to please

You became so involved in my success

Even put all your dreams to the side as I pursued my quest

All these sacrifices that you did for me

Made me feel like I could not tell you who I want to be

So afraid to offend you if I spoke my mind

Pure fear creeping up and down my spine

It's like asking someone to do an impossible task

Long before COVID-19, I had always worn a mask

The mere thought that your love might disappear

Forces me to put on many masks that will cause you to smile and cheer

I tried to take it off once to play a little trick

Then the look on your face was so disappointing that I had to stop it quick

Knowing I would have to conform back to your point of view

Maybe you will find out my interests if I keep throwing clues

Now I am running out of time to find my own two shoes

Regretting the fact that I did not say I did it all for you

POINTS OF REFLECTION

1. Have you ever put your dreams to the side to please someone else? Explain.

2. What kept you from expressing your true thoughts and feelings to that person?

3. Did you have any regrets later in life? Share.

4. Think of someone you know who may struggle with desires to please others. Express three to five ways you might encourage that person to follow their dreams.

ADDITIONAL THOUGHTS AND COMMENTS:

WORD SEARCH

They say stick and stones may break my bones, but words will never hurt me

I have always wondered within my mind one's rationale for cursing

Does it make a person feel like they are full grown

Maybe it's still a young child trying to come into their own

Are we really using these words as a form of protection?

Masking an underlying belief that we must walk around with a constant erection

Is it that we can't find the right words to say

Expressing deep-seated emotions trying to make someone pay

Overused throughout entirety while losing our way to express

Misrepresentations of its usage, vying like it's a birthright to success

They can't tell me what to say – it's my freedom of expression

So blinded by our own ignorance while disregarding the lesson

Freedom of expression sounds all great in theory

Until your expressions start to disturb the peace of humanity

Building up your vocab is my main confession

Empower yourself to move from the back row to the VIP section

POINTS OF REFLECTION

1. Do you curse? If so, what is your reason for cursing?

2. What makes it difficult for you to find alternative words to say?

3. Are there any people or locations that make you more aware or prevent your use of curse words?

4. Who do you feel is influenced the most by the words you choose to use?

5. Share three to five things you can do to decrease your use of curse words.

ADDITIONAL THOUGHTS AND COMMENTS:

CHILDISH GAMES

Is being childish the key to one's success

I know it sounds ridiculous, but there is something that I must confess

Could this be the game changer that you always wanted to see

Or maybe someone blowing smoke and selling pipedreams

So, let's take a moment to introspect

About some childish qualities you probably won't expect

At a young age, we were fueled by our own imagination

The process of growing up has caused our mind to endure severe constipation

Fearless to the ways of how things worked on Earth

Only caring about the rules of the games while making sure we come in first

Overwhelming confidence in our own abilities

Now we question our every move, a plague of insecurity

Socializing on playgrounds and getting things off our chest

Seems like the only communication going on now involves a video or a

text

Going back to the basics has many individuals concerned

But it was the optimal time that we were primed to learn

Not so focused on who was teaching the lesson

Obtaining new knowledge while adults treat it like indigestion

I know you had a rough life, but I am going to keep it simple

It's kind of hard to succeed at anything without fundamentals

Hopefully, I said enough to allow your mind to dissect

Even the greatest at their craft don't let basic experience neglect

The simplicity of this concept can sound wild

For the key to success is connecting back with that inner child

POINTS OF REFLECTION

1. What do you think of the idea of being childish as the key to success?

2. How have some of your childhood dreams changed as you got older?

3. What role does fear play in your ability to achieve success?

4. State three to five ways you can start reconnecting to that fearless inner child.

ADDITIONAL THOUGHTS AND COMMENTS:

WAR WOUNDS

Every soldier has a story to tell

Recalling the origins with all the minor details

Telling everyone about the blasts from the past

Overshadowing the scars like a sunny day with severe overcast

These scars you see serve as living proof

That no one walks through life without war wounds

Some scars are visible to the naked eye

But most are buried deep down inside

Hoping to never see the light of day

The very thought of being vulnerable just takes my breath away

I see how society can rip a person's life into shreds

Modern day version of being tarred with feathers all over your head

Therefore, I prefer to remain emotionally silent

Fearing that all these emotions unleashed will equal to violence

How would I put a cap back on this bottomless well

Knowing all paths lead to an institution or a cell

One day I decided there was so much more to me

These scars became beautiful and were meant for everyone to see

They serve as a testament to all my blessings

Like a vehicular checkup that continues to pass inspection

So, soldiers take pride in all the stories you tell

Because your war wounds could be the key to getting someone else out of

mental jail

POINTS OF REFLECTION

1. How do you hide your war wounds from the past?

2. What are some of your biggest fears about being vulnerable?

3. Have you ever been able to see the beauty in your battle scars? Explain.

4. List three positive statements that can encourage others to identify the beauty in their war wounds.

ADDITIONAL THOUGHTS AND COMMENTS:

BLURRED VISION

Everyone's looking for that magic falling from the skies

Looking for that special something to help them galvanize

Eager to find that power that has helped so many people rise

Distracted by the evils of this world as if they were hypnotized

Captivated by how others seem to achieve elevation

While baffled by how their own efforts lead to mere stagnation

There must be an easy way, so we start taking shortcuts

Finding ourselves back in the same situation with all the if's and but's

Refusing to take the time to plan our attack with precision

Minimizing the fact that there is no plan without adequate vision

Vision is the process of how our plans and actions align

Its absence is like driving to a new destination choosing to ignore all the

traffic signs

A vision starts in the mind then becomes reality

Ever seen an architect start building without a blueprint — Pure insanity

The lack of traction can make any sane person feel perturbed

Impulsivity has caused many individuals' vision to become blurred

The answer lies in your very selection

Are you doing it for selfish reasons or for the greater good with divine protection

You are meant to do extraordinary things, and this is no mistake

Make your dreams bigger than you to become one of the greats

POINTS OF REFLECTION

1. How can you tell when your vision is blurred?

2. Have you ever tried to take shortcuts to avoid necessary lessons? Share.

3. Do your dreams ever seem so big that they scare you? Explain.

4. List three to five quotes or philosophies that help keep your vision less blurry.

ADDITIONAL THOUGHTS AND COMMENTS:

CLOSURE

It's like trying to close a door with someone's foot in it

Losing track of how it all begun, just want it to be finished

Thought you were behind me, but you keep coming over

Just like an addiction... hard to stay sober

I tell myself not to think about it or just let it go

Time heals all wounds, but it's like something is blocking my growth

Carrying all this weight around... got me moving slow

This is my real life, not a reality show

Trying to move on... can I find a witness

But I can't forget the most important element called, "forgiveness"

Forgiveness is the process of humbling oneself

While gaining the courage to push through circumstances even if our

attempts go deaf

Understanding that each person may feel like they are being attacked

Sometimes being the bigger person feels like a cell phone getting hacked

Most importantly, take the first step in the process to regain your composure

'Cause every end has a new beginning through this thing called, "closure"

POINTS OF REFLECTION

1. How hard is it for you to get closure with things and/or people?

2. What usually keeps you from turning the page and moving on to the next chapter?

3. When you hear the word *forgiveness*, what comes to your mind?

4. Have you ever forgiven someone or asked for forgiveness? Which was more difficult?

5. Identify three to five ways you can start enjoying new beginnings.

ADDITIONAL THOUGHTS AND COMMENTS:

A WORD FROM THE AUTHOR

The metaphorical messages in this book
have caused me to search for deeper understanding.

They reflect the struggles of many while providing
an effective response to work toward meaningful solutions.

May these words provide you with encouragement
to challenge the conventional logic that blocks you
from making lasting changes in your life.

-Roderick Hambrick ("The Acronymist")

Also available on Kindle.